Disclaimer Notice: You must take note that the information in this document is for casual reading and entertainment purposes only. We have made every attempt to provide accurate, up- todate, and reliable information. We do not express or imply guarantees of any kind. The persons who read admit that the writer is not occupied in giving legal, financial, medical, or other advice. We put this book content by sourcing various places.

Please consult a licensed professional before you try any techniques shown in this book. By going through this document, the book lover comes to an agreement that under no situation is the author accountable for any forfeiture, direct or indirect, which they may incur because of the use of material contained in this document, including, but not limited to, α errors, omissions, or inaccuracies

COLOR TEST PAGE

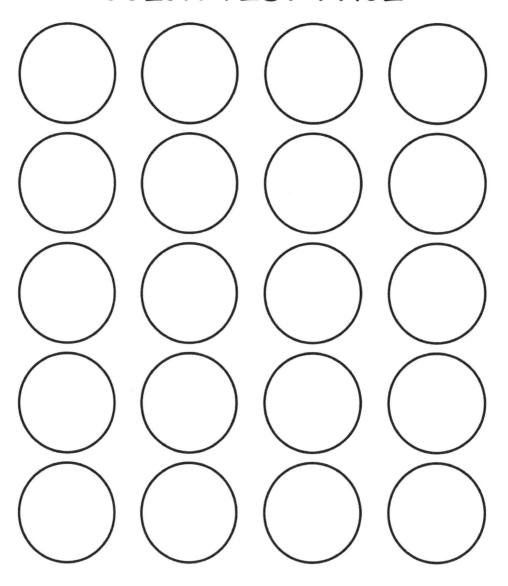

UNITED STATES

CANADA

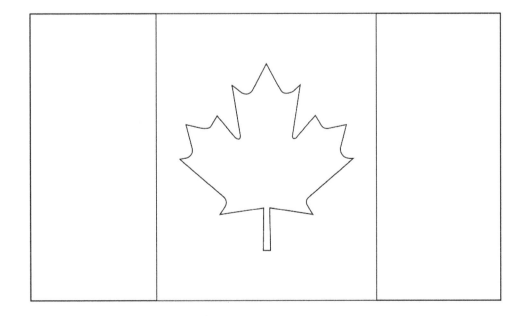

JAMAICA

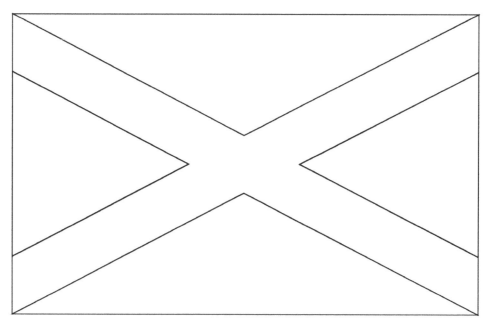

MEXICO

CUBA

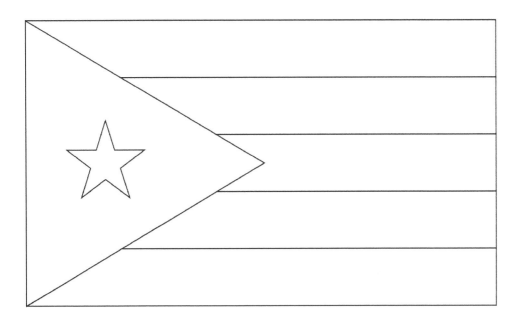

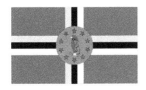

DOMINICA

 ANTIGUA AND BARBUDA

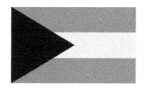 BAHAMAS

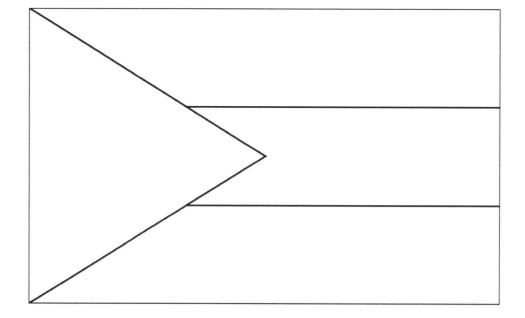

BARBADOS

TRINIDAD AND TOBAGO

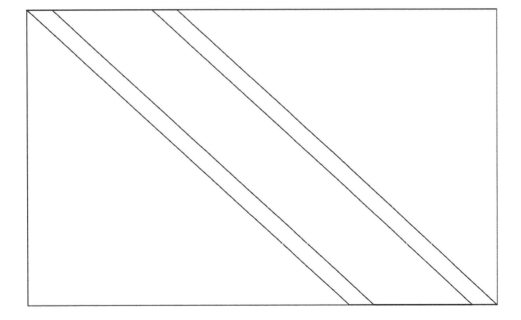

NICARAGUA

COSTA RICA

GRENADA

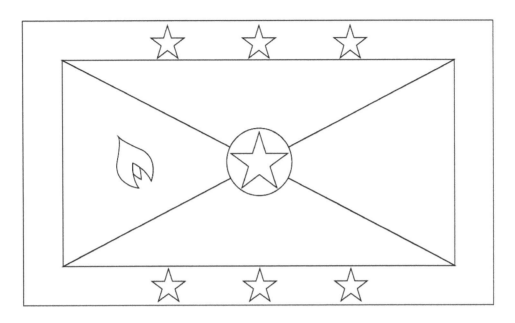

GREENLAND

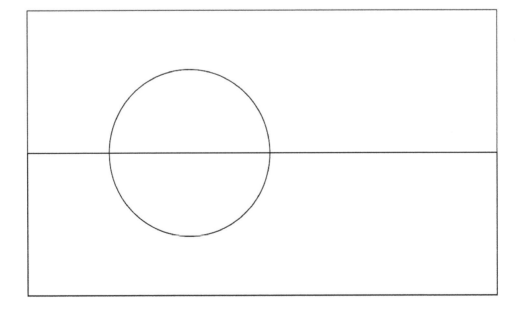

GUATEMALA

HAITI

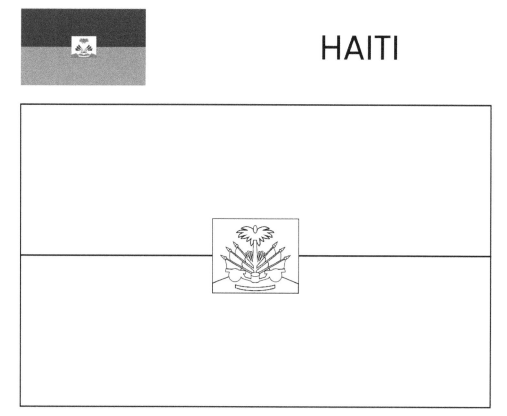

HONDURAS

PANAMA

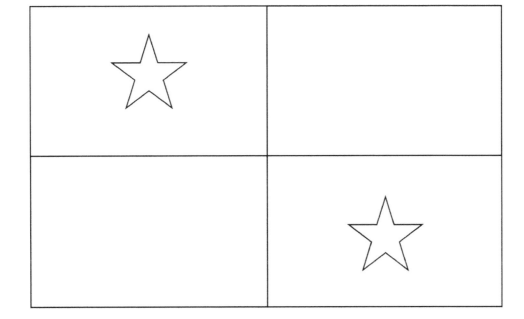

 SAINT LUCIA

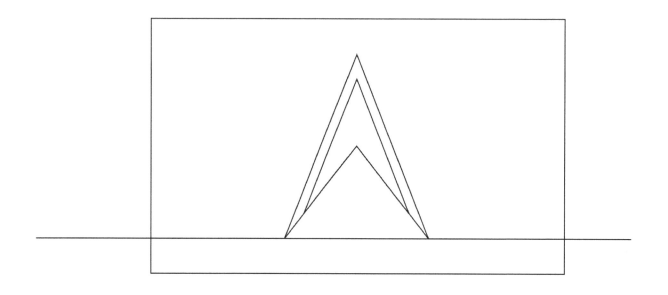

 SAINT KITTS AND NEVIS

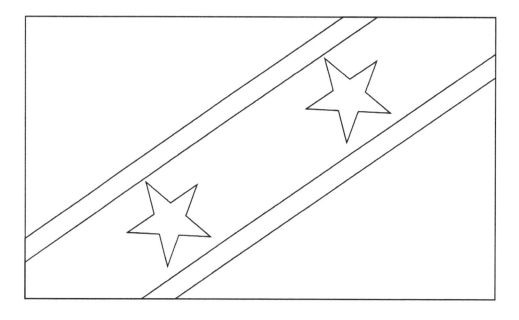

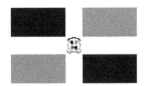

DOMINICAN REPUBLIC

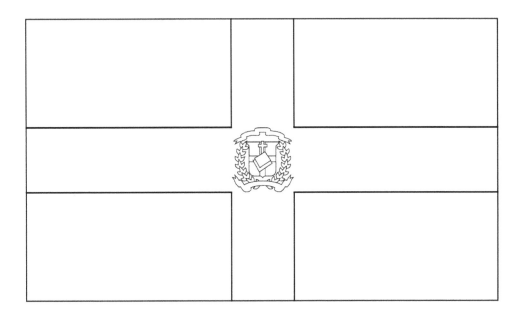

SAINT VINCENT
AND THE GRENADINES

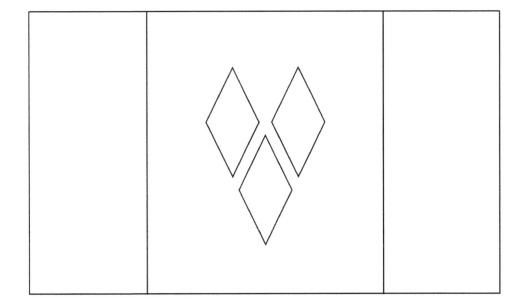

 # PUERTO RICO

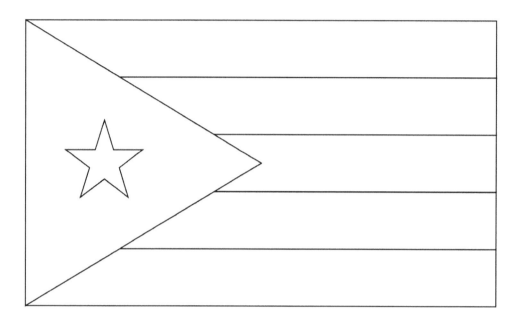

 # EL SALVADOR

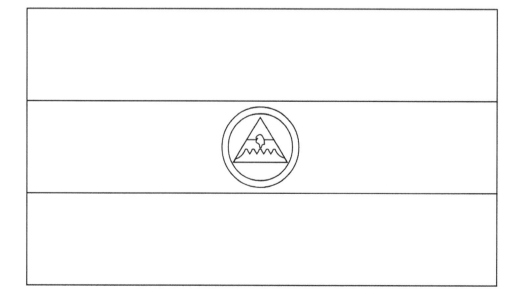

ARGENTINA

BRAZIL

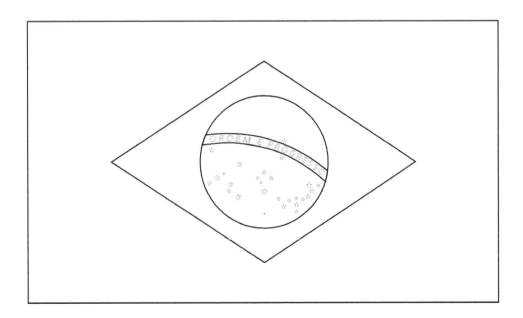

PARAGUAY

BOLIVIA

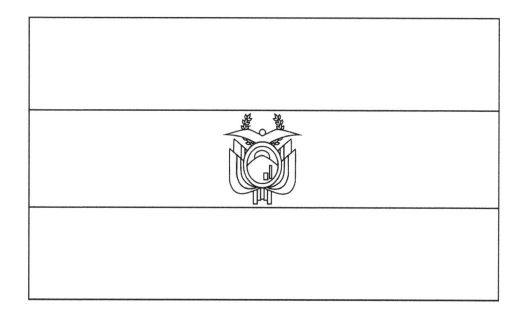

 URUGUAY

 ECUADOR

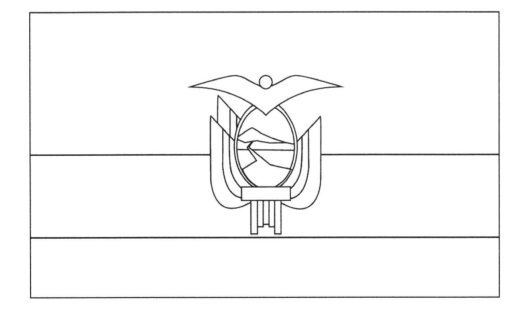

COLOMBIA

CHILE

PERU

VENEZUELA

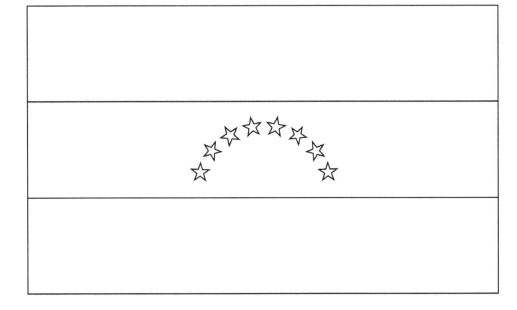

AUSTRALIA

SAMOA

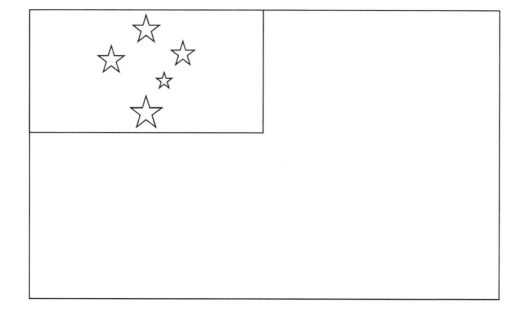

 # KIRIBATI

 # SOLOMON ISLANDS

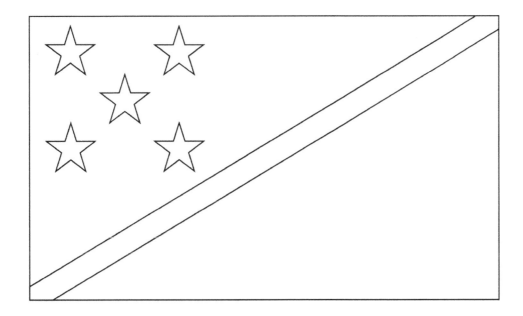

 MARSHALL ISLANDS

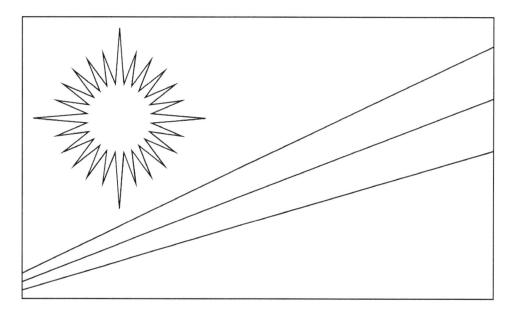

 MICRONESIA

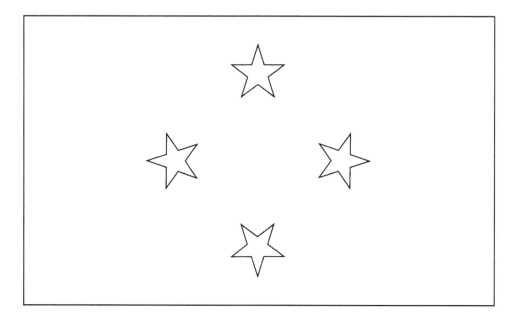

VANUATU

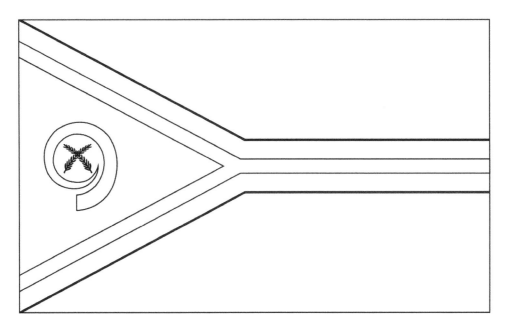

NEW ZEALAND

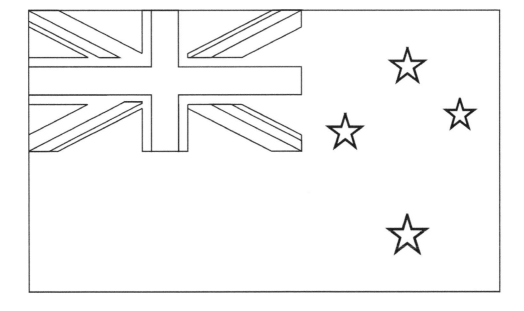

PALAU

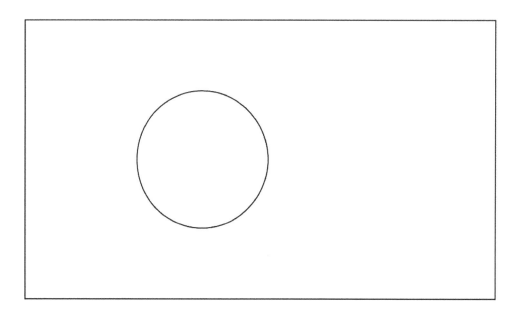

PAPUA NEW GUINEA

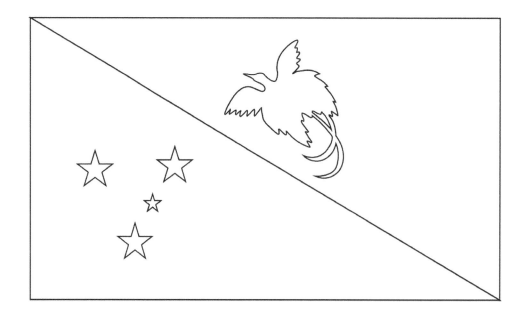

NAURU

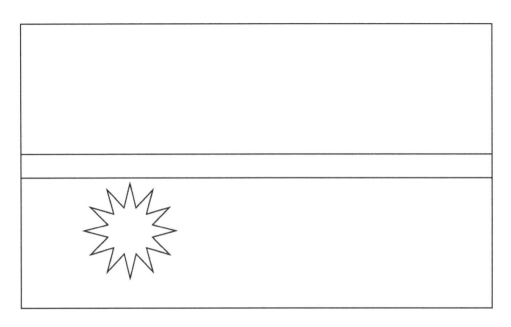

FIJI

TUVALU

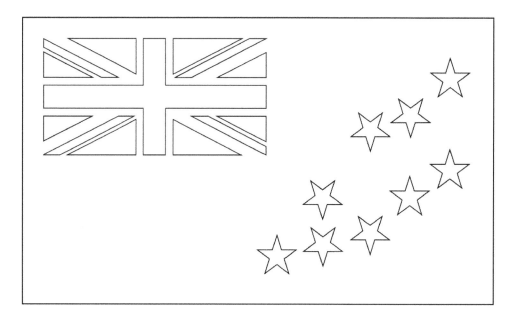

TONGA

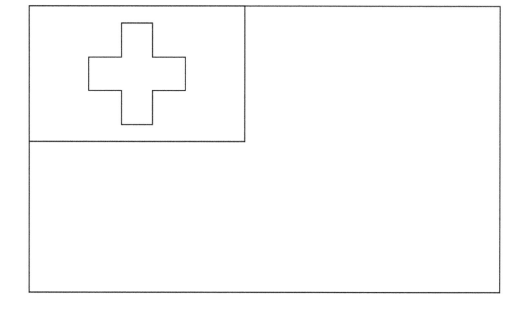

ALBANIA

ANDORRA

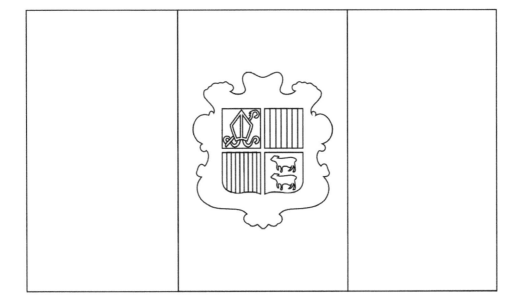

CROATIA

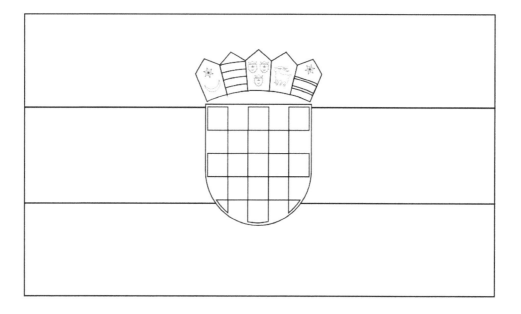

BELARUS

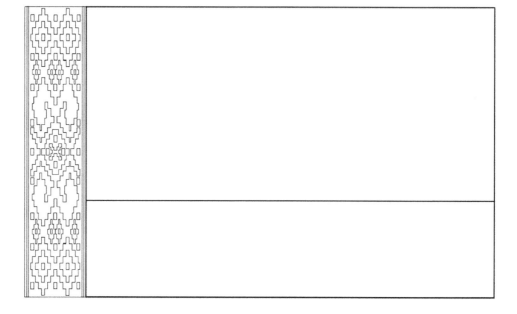

 # GEORGIA

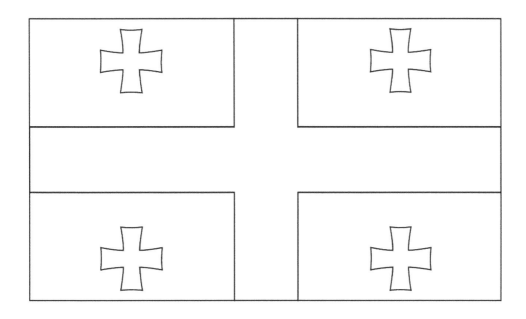

 # CYPRUS

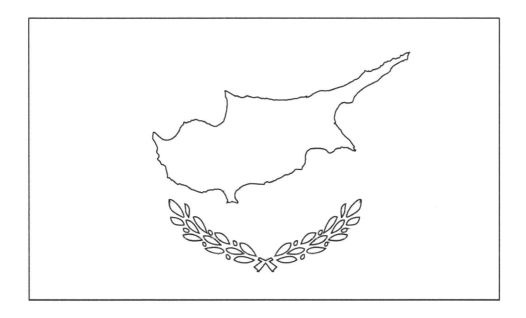

KOSOVO

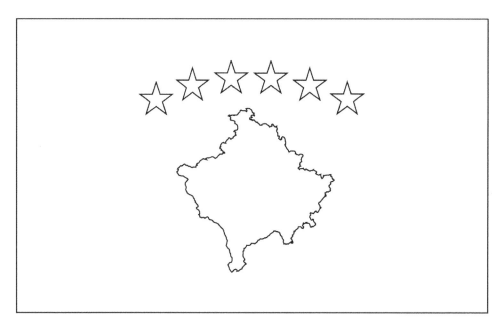

LIECHTENSTEIN

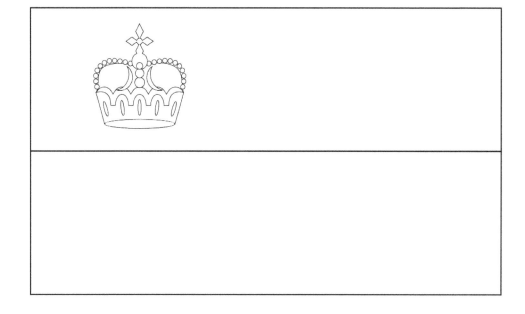

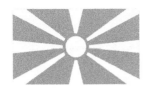 MACEDONIA

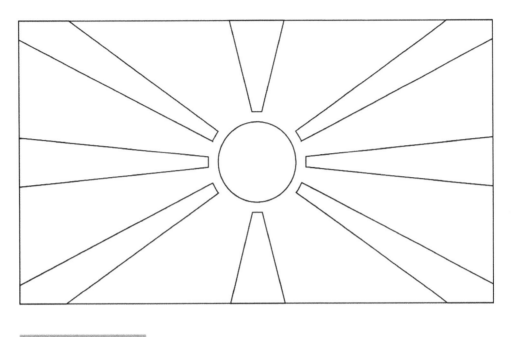

LUXEMBOURG

MONTENEGRO

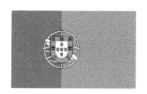

PORTUGAL

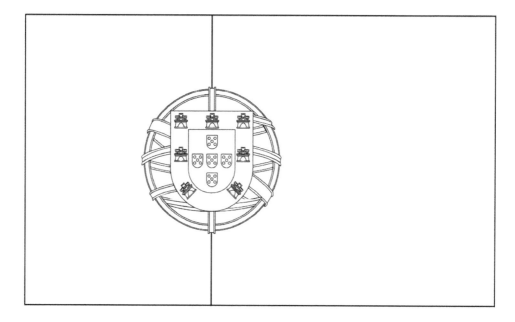

RUSSIA

SAN MARINO

 SERBIA

 SLOVENIA

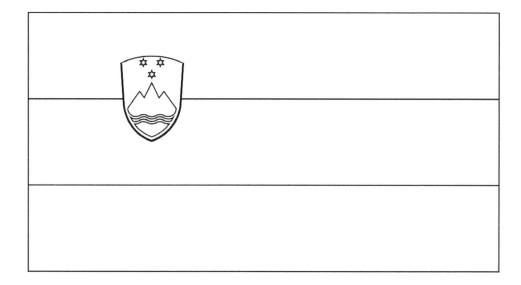

SPAIN

ARMENIA

AUSTRIA

AZERBAIJAN

 # BOSNIA AND HERZEGOVINA

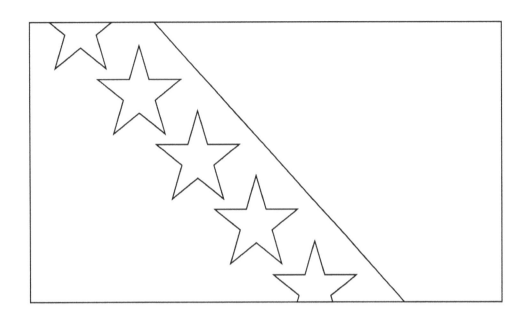

 # BELGIUM

DENMARK

BULGARIA

FINLAND

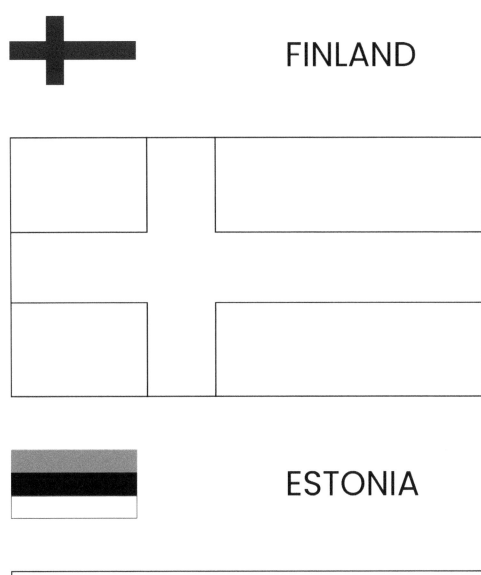

ESTONIA

FRANCE

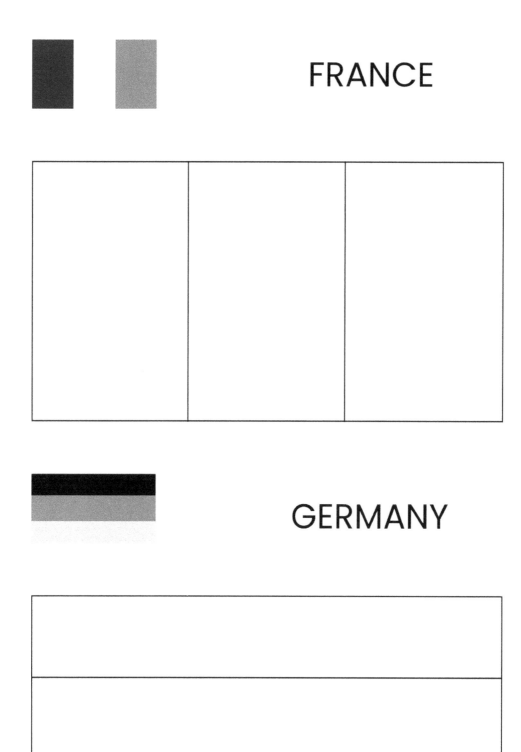

GERMANY

HUNGARY

GREECE

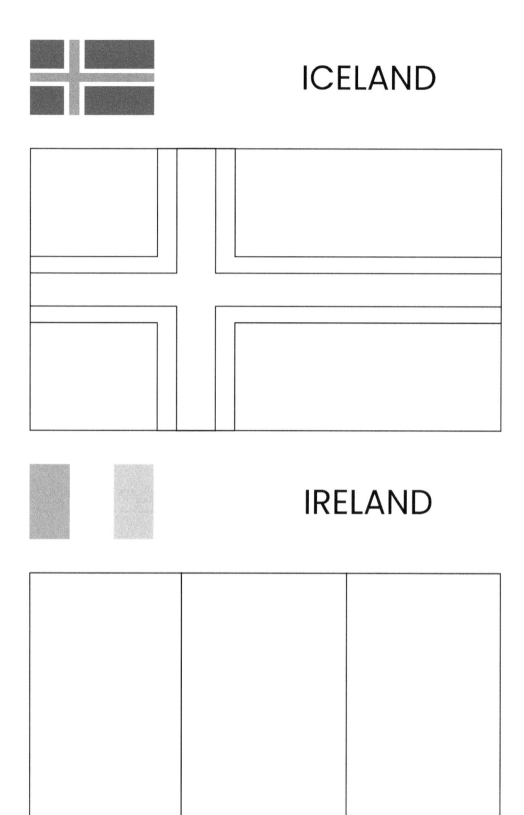

ICELAND

IRELAND

ITALY

KAZAKHSTAN

LATVIA

LITHUANIA

MOLDOVA

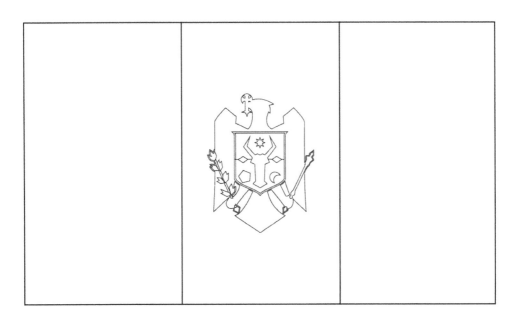

MALTA

SLOVAKIA

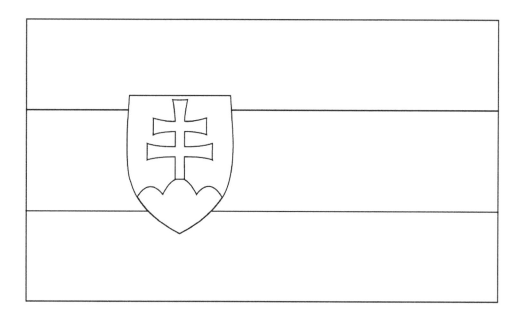

SWEDEN

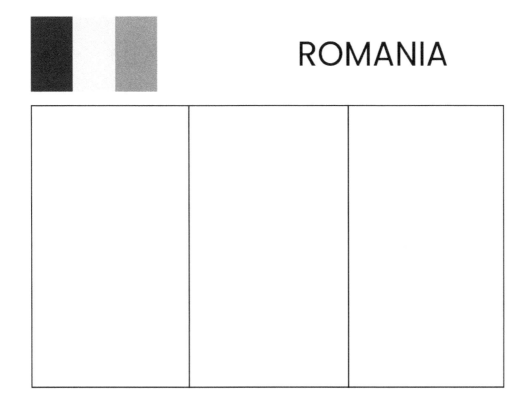

ROMANIA

SWITZERLAND

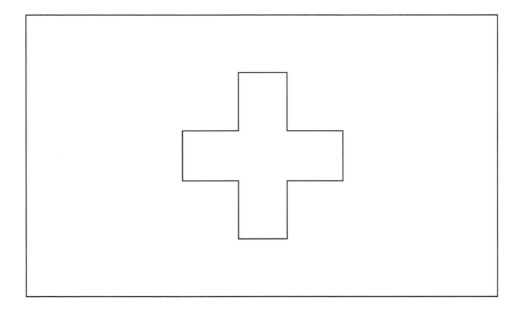

TURKEY

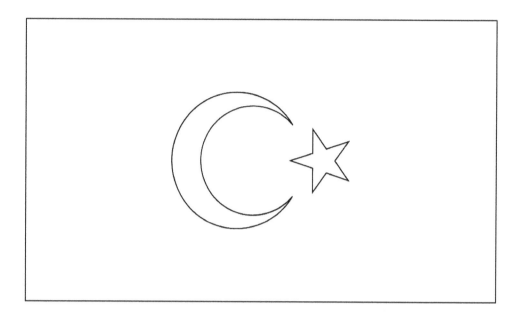

UKRAINE

CZECHIA

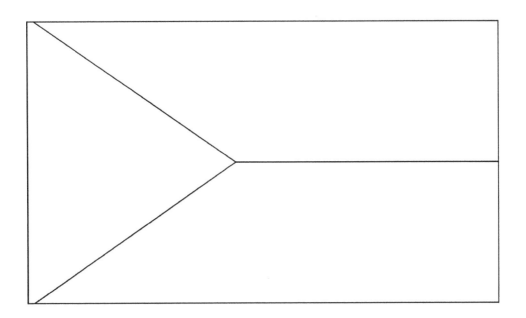

UNITED KINGDOM

NETHERLANDS

NORWAY

SCOTLAND

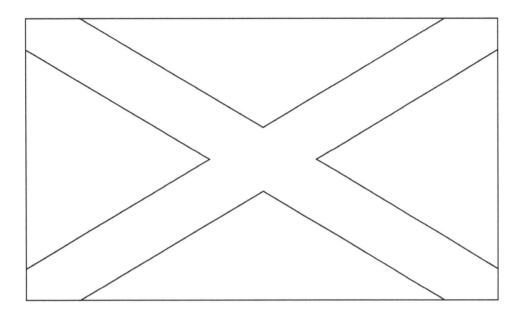

WALES

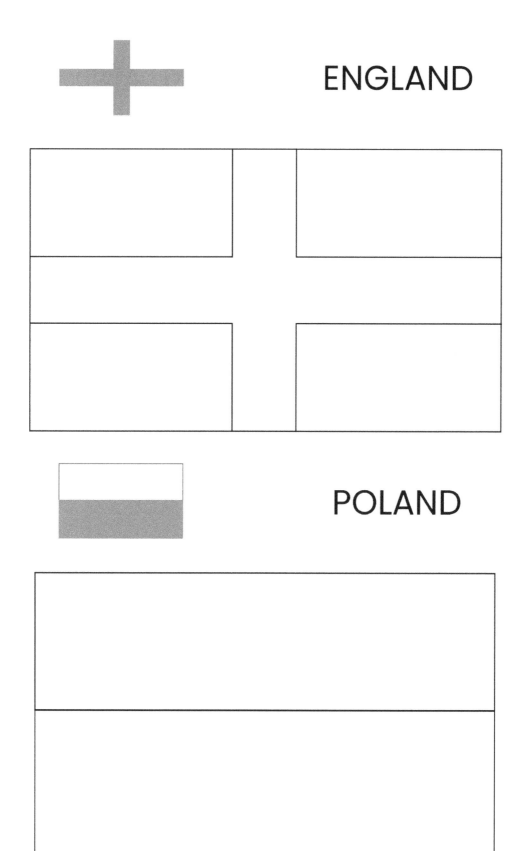

ENGLAND

POLAND

ALGERIA

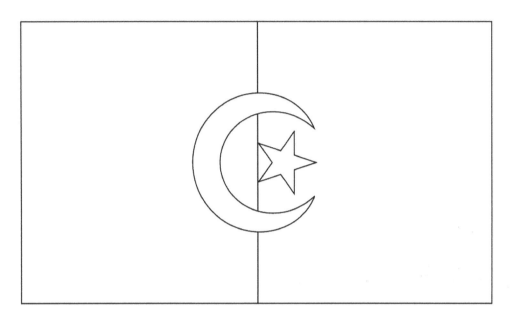

 ANGOLA

BOTSWANA

BENIN

BURUNDI

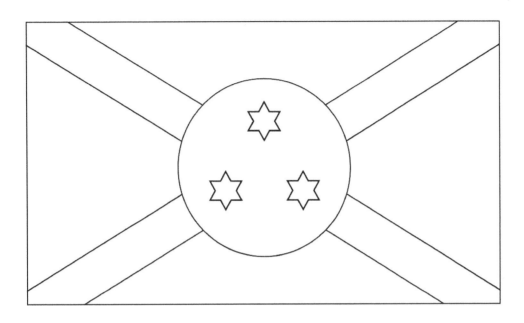

BURKINA FASO

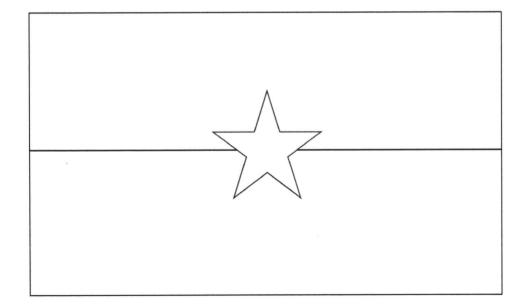

CENTRAL
AFRICAN REPUBLIC

CAMEROON

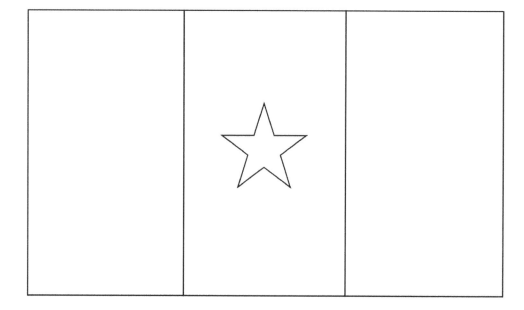

COMOROS

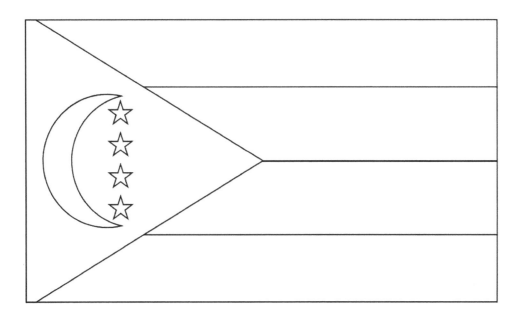

CHAD

CONGO REPUBLIC

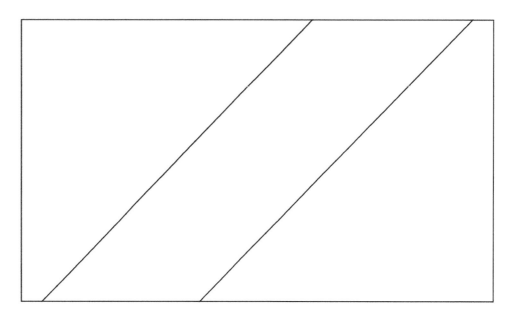

CONGO

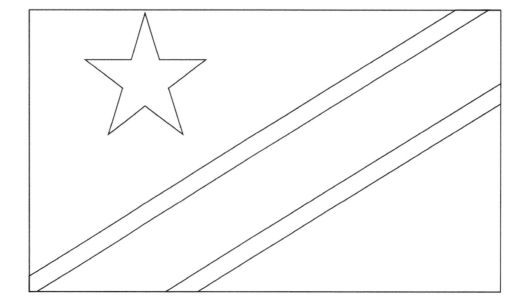

EGYPT

IVORY COAST

DJIBOUTI

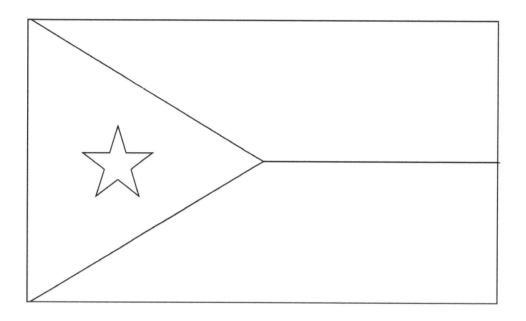

ERITREA

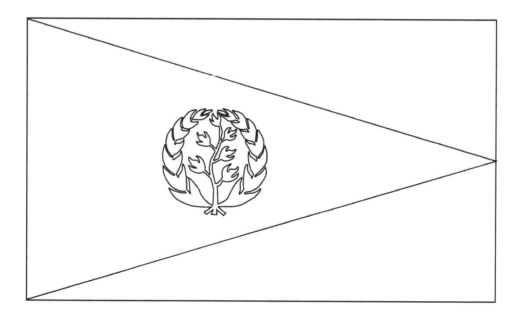

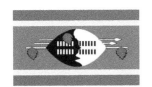

ESWATINI

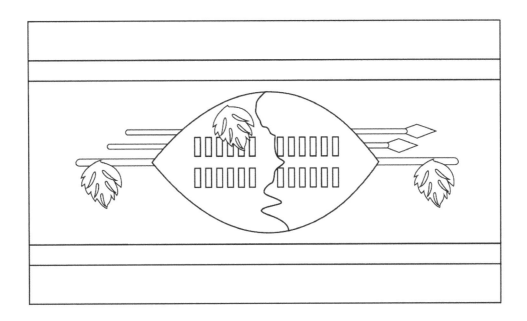

ETHIOPIA

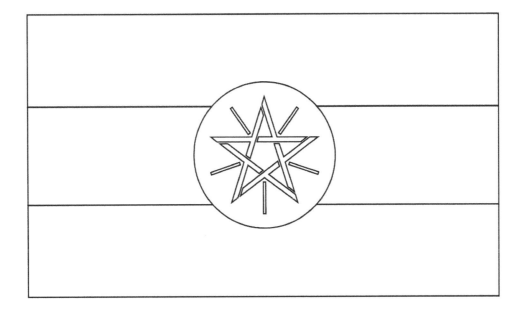

GABON

GAMBIA

GUINEA

GHANA

MADAGASCAR

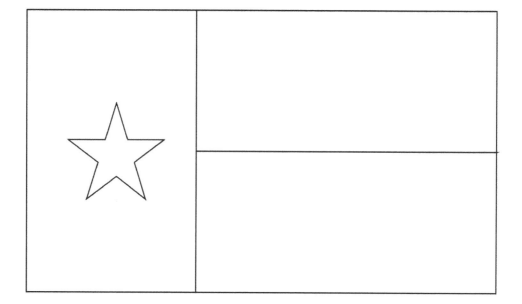

GUINEA BISSAU

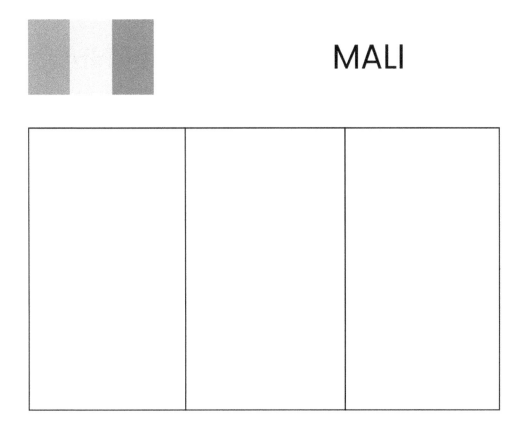

MALI

MALAWI

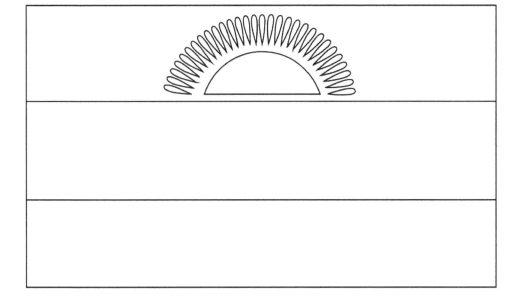

MAURITANIA

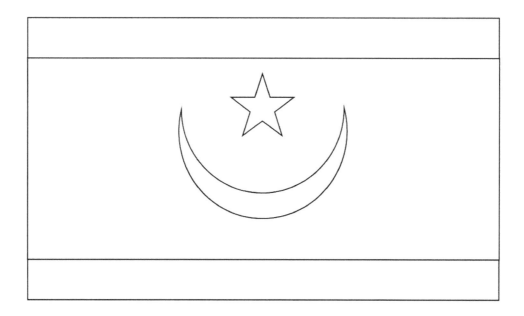

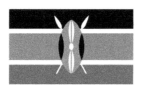

KENYA

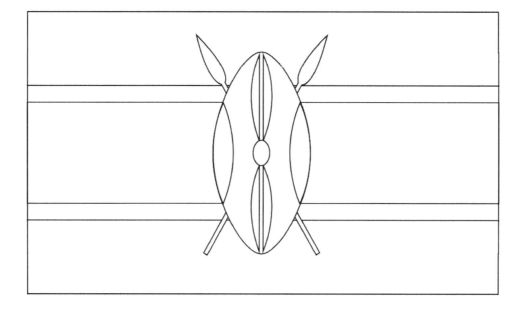

MOROCCO

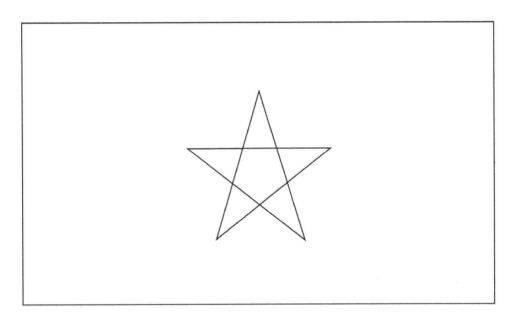

MOZAMBIQUE

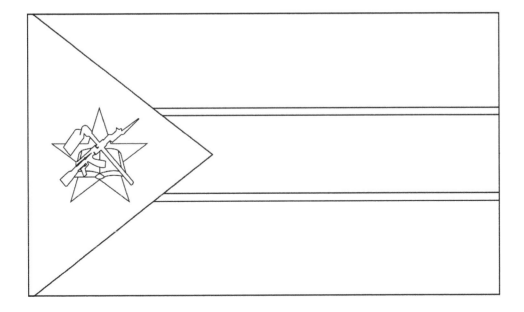

LESOTHO

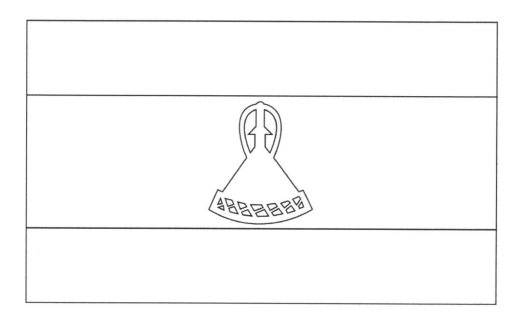

NAMIBIA

LIBERIA

LIBYA

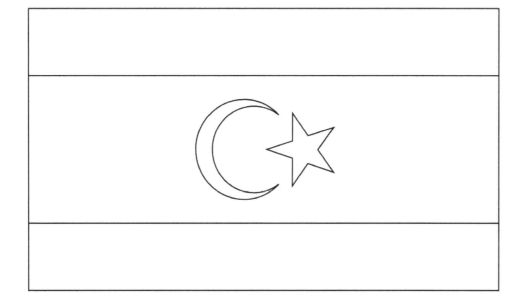

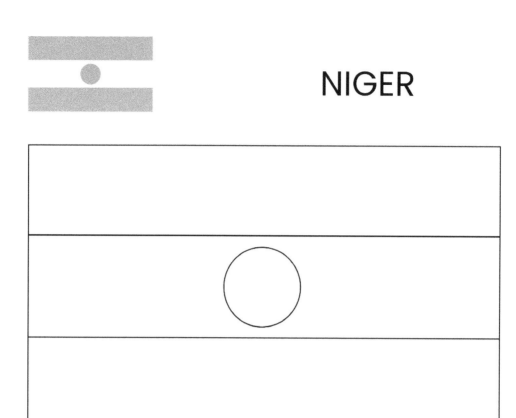

NIGER

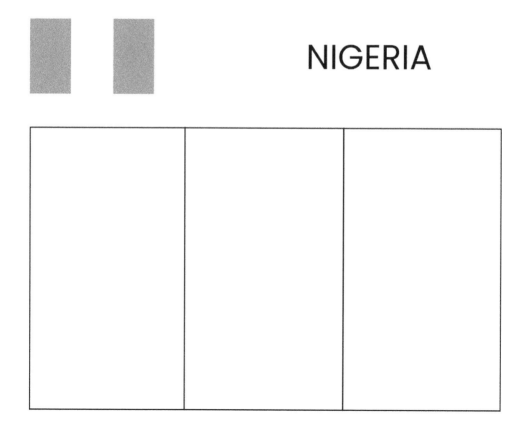

NIGERIA

 SAO TOME

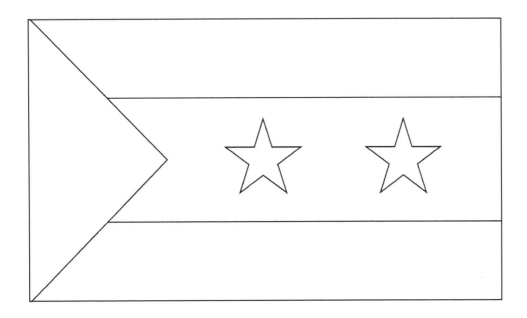

 RWANDA

MAURITIUS

SENEGAL

TOGO

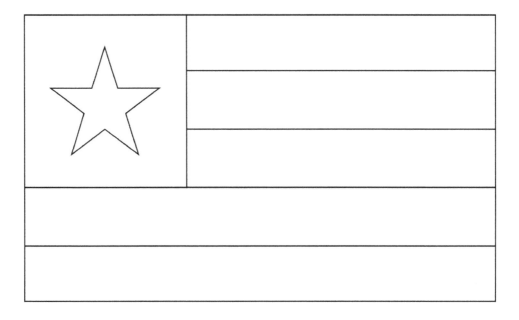

SEYCHELLES

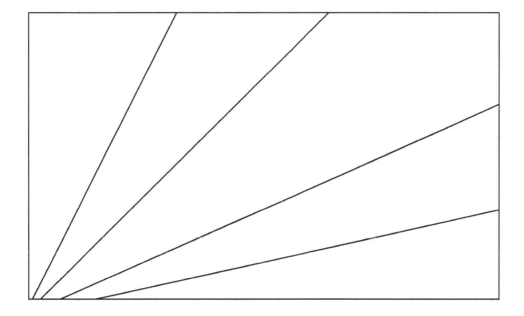

SIERRA LEONE

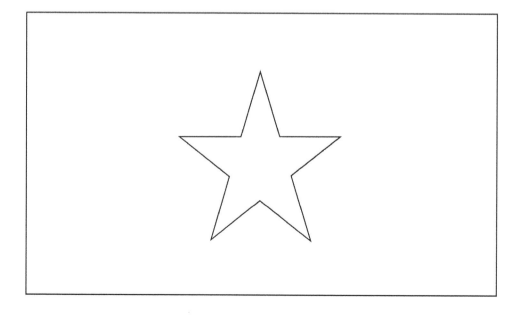

SOMALIA

SOUTH AFRICA

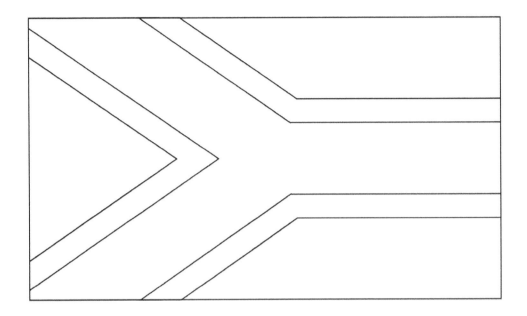

SOUTH SUDAN

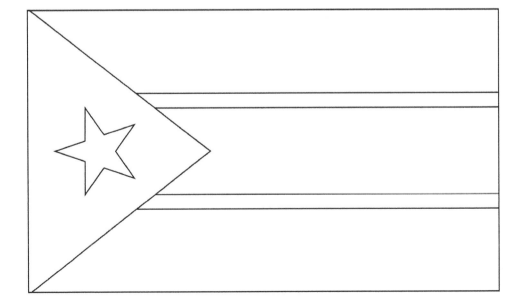

SUDAN

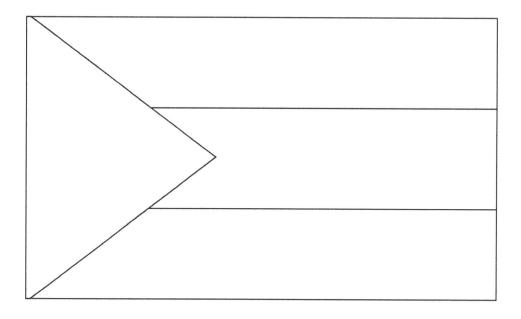

TANZANIA

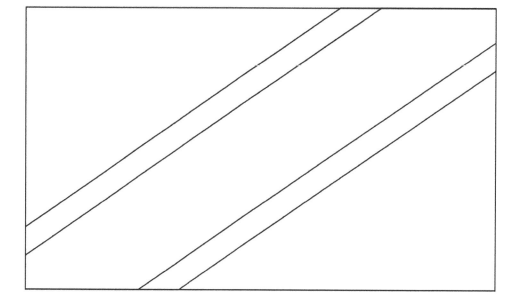

 TUNISIA

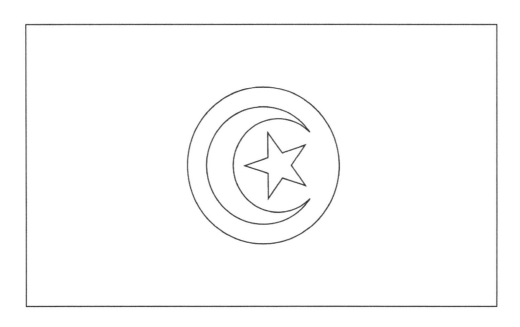

 UGANDA

ZIMBABWE

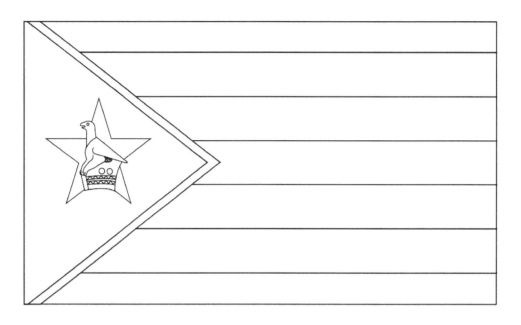

ZAMBIA

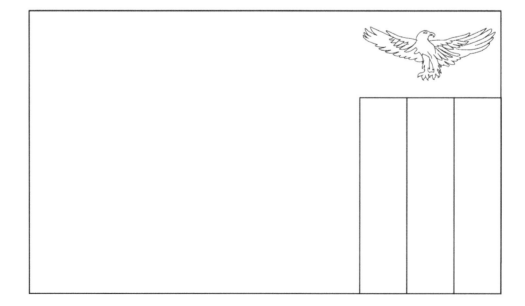

EQUATORIAL GUINEA

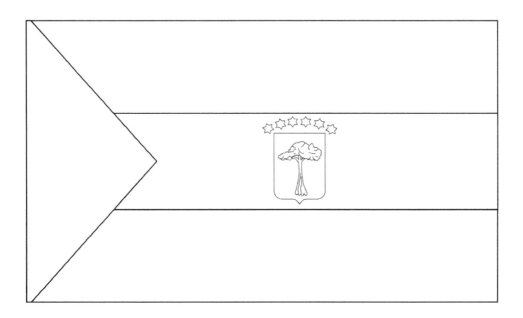

CABO VERDE

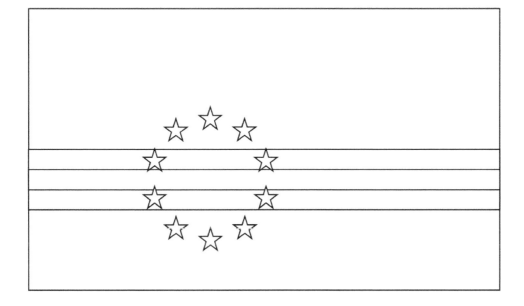

AZERBAIJAN

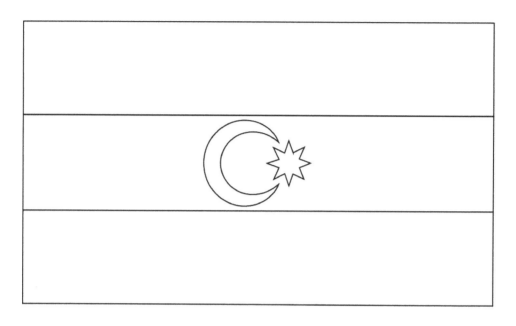

TURKMENISTAN

BANGLADESH

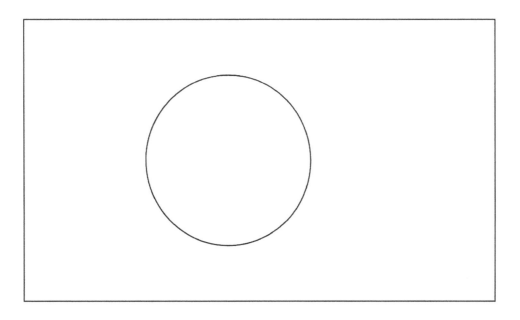

BAHRAIN

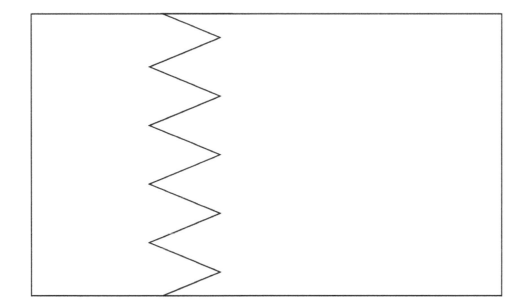

BRUNEI

BHUTAN

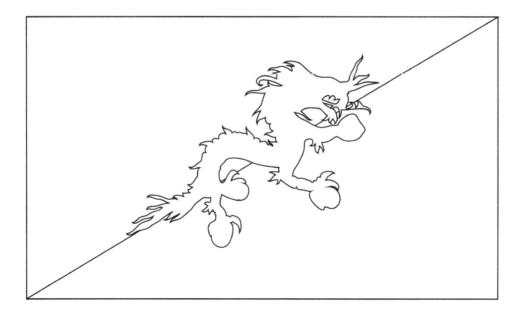

CHINA

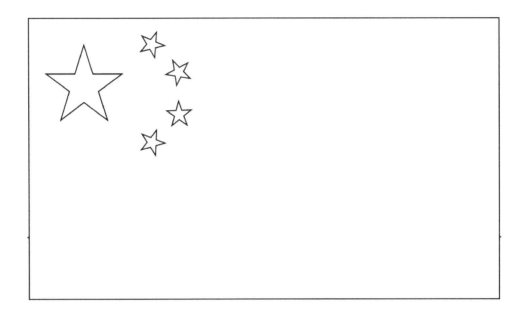

CAMBODIA

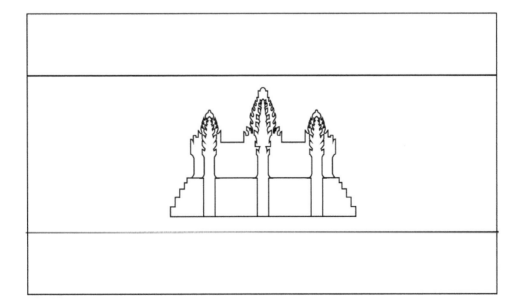

UZBEKISTAN

UNITED ARAB EMIRATES

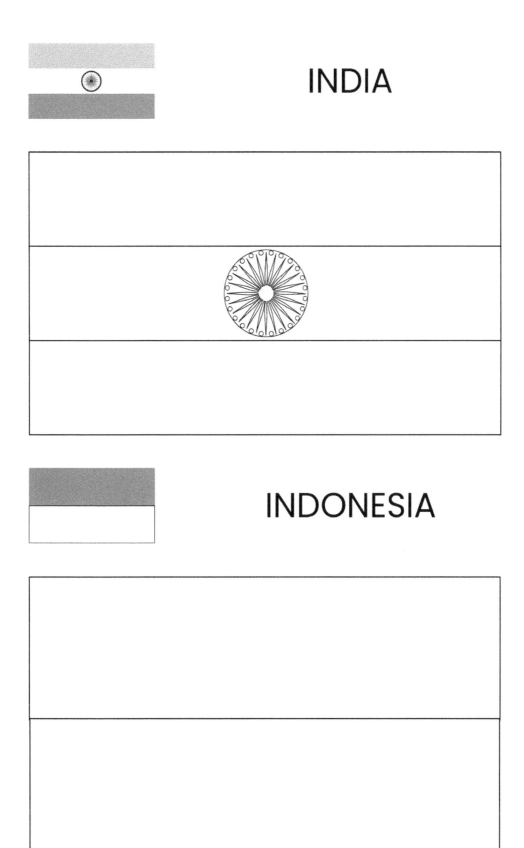

INDIA

INDONESIA

IRAQ

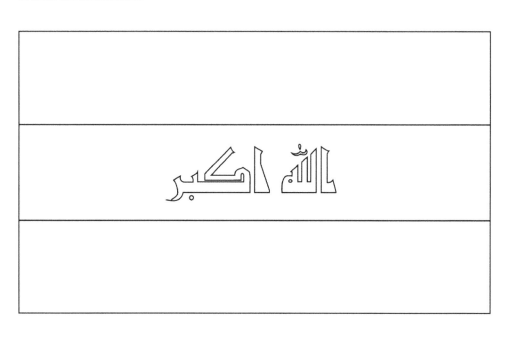

IRAN

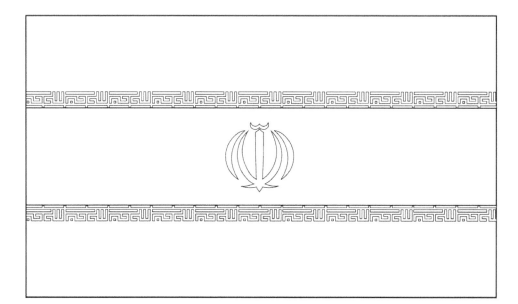

JAPAN

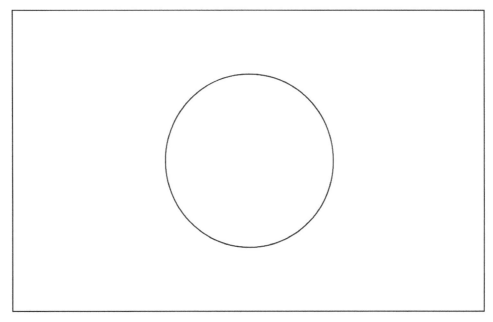

JORDAN

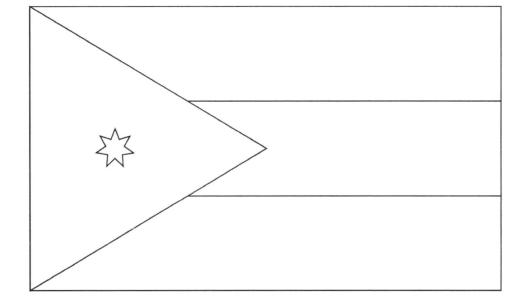

KUWAIT

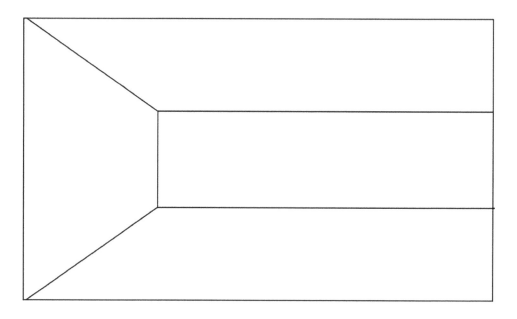

KYRGYZSTAN

LEBANON

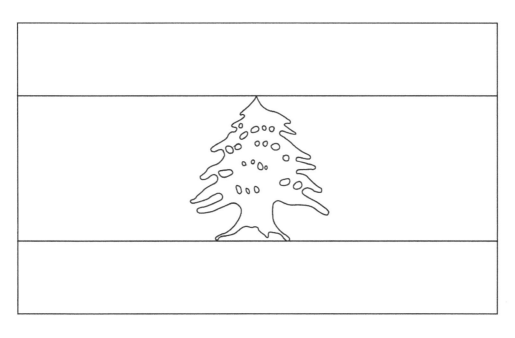

LAOS

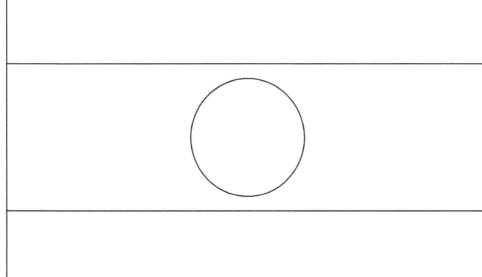

MALAYSIA

MALDIVES

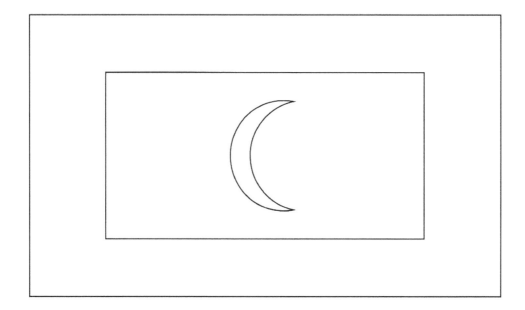

VIETNAM

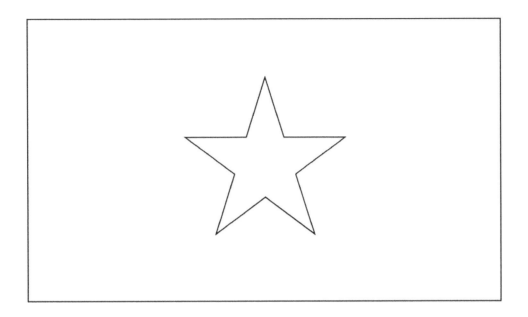

MYANMAR

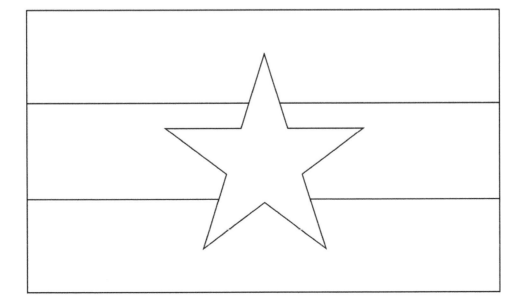

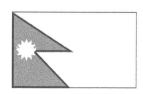

NEPAL

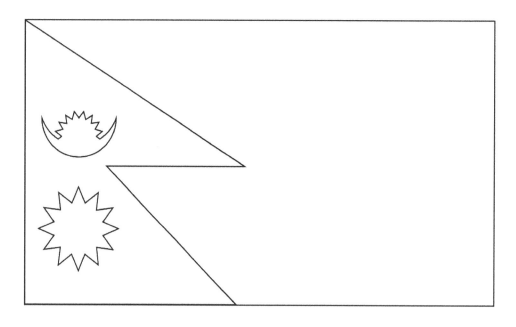

NORTH KOREA

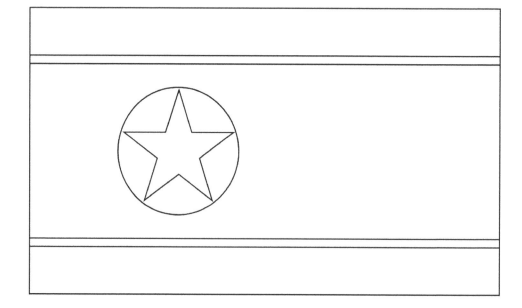

PAKISTAN

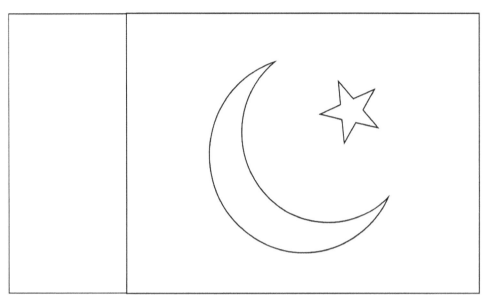

OMAN

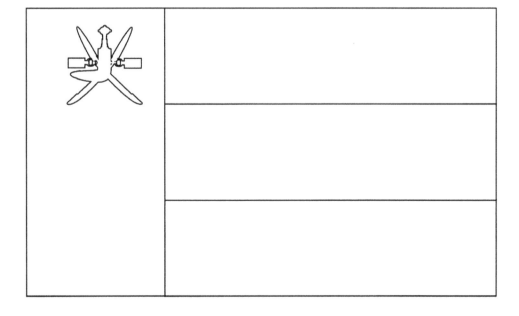

PHILIPPINES

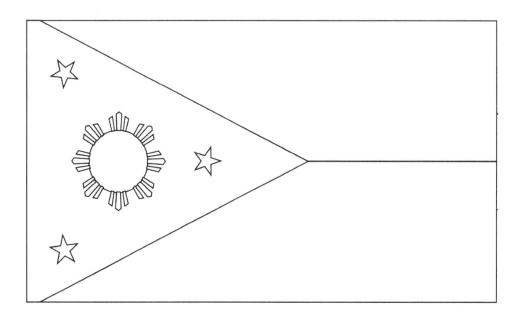

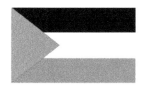

PALESTINE

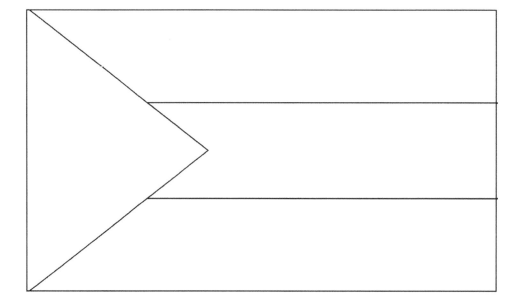

QATAR

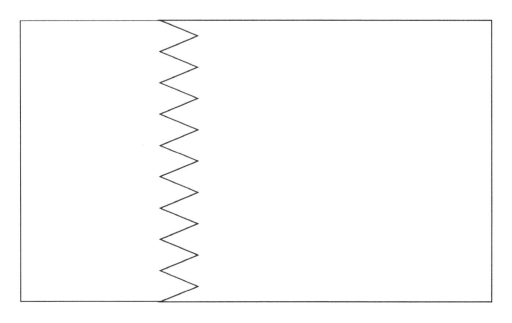

SAUDI ARABIA

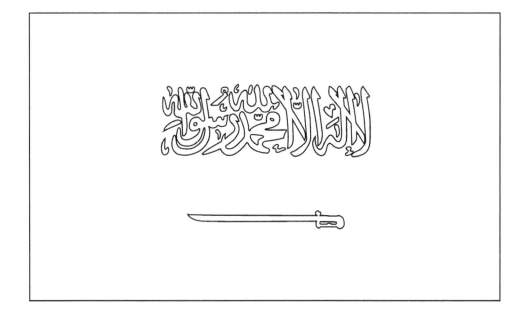

 # SINGAPORE

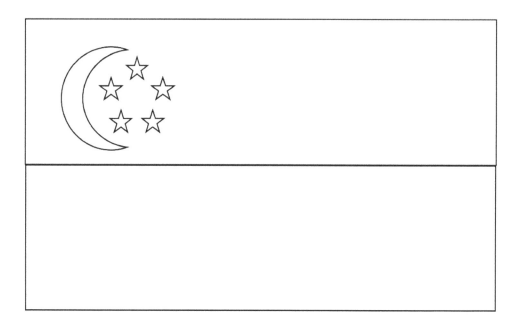

 # SOUTH KOREA

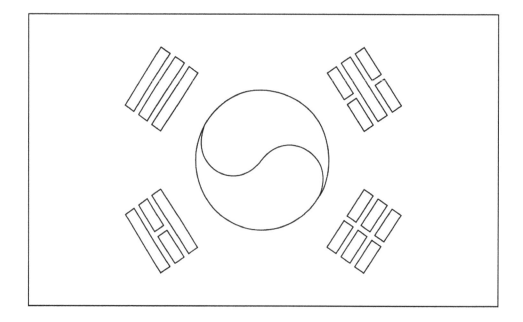

SYRIA

SRI LANKA

 TAIWAN

TAJIKISTAN

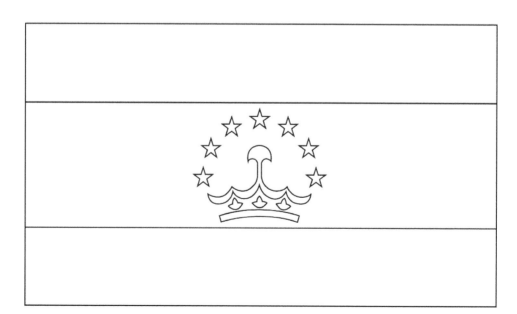

THAILAND

TIMOR LESTE

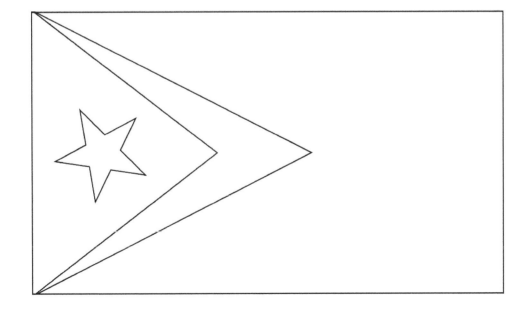

YEMEN

AFGHANISTAN

MONGOLIA

Thank You

Please share your feedback on our book.

Your opinion is important to us as a small family business.

Thank you! Please let us know how you like our book at:

 contact@georgicasworld.com

Ingram Content Group UK Ltd.
Milton Keynes UK
UKHW050758070623
423023UK00008B/485